ZENDAYA

BY MARY BLECKWEHL

AMICUS LEARNING

Inspire is published by
Amicus Learning, an imprint of Amicus
P.O. Box 227
Mankato, MN 56002
www.amicuspublishing.us

Copyright © 2025 Amicus.
International copyright reserved in all countries.
No part of this book may be reproduced in any form
without written permission from the publisher.

Editor: Ana Brauer
Series Designer: Kathleen Petelinsek
Book Designer and Photo Researcher: Emily Dietz

Library of Congress Cataloging-in-Publication Data
Names: Bleckwehl, Mary E., author.
Title: Zendaya / by Mary Bleckwehl.
Description: Mankato, MN : Amicus Learning, an imprint of Amicus, 2025. | Series: Inspire | Includes bibliographical references and index. | Audience: Ages 5-9 | Audience: Grades 2-3 | Summary: "Learn about actress and singer Zendaya and how she paved her way to Hollywood in this biography packed with photos and fact-filled text suitable for young readers. Includes a table of contents, glossary, further resources, and index"— Provided by publisher.
Identifiers: LCCN 2024012077 (print) | LCCN 2024012078 (ebook) | ISBN 9798892001083 (library binding) | ISBN 9798892001663 (paperback) | ISBN 9798892002240 (ebook)
Subjects: LCSH: Zendaya, 1996—Juvenile literature. | Actors—United States—Biography—Juvenile literature. | Singers—United States—Biography—Juvenile literature. | LCGFT: Biographies.
Classification: LCC PN2287.Z47 B53 2025 (print) | LCC PN2287.Z47 (ebook) | DDC 791.4302/8092 [B]—dc23/eng/20240326
LC record available at https://lccn.loc.gov/2024012077
LC ebook record available at https://lccn.loc.gov/2024012078

Photo Credits: Alamy Stock Photo/Album, 10, Sthanlee B. Mirador/Sipa USA, cover, WENN, 18; AP Images/ Eric Charbonneau, 14; Getty Images/ALFREDO ESTRELLA, 20, Daniele Venturelli, 5, Debra L Rothenberg, 12, FREDERIC J. BROWN, 16, Michael Buckner, 13, Patrick McMullan, 9, San Francisco Chronicle/Hearst Newspapers, 6, The Chosunilbo JNS, 19; Shutterstock/Lightspring, 8, Viktor Hladchenko, 15

Printed in China

Table of Contents

- 4 **From Shy to Stardom**
- 7 **Bit by the Acting Bug**
- 8 **Chasing Her Dream**
- 11 **Finding Fame**
- 12 **Music Star**
- 15 **Leap to the Big Screen**
- 17 **Leading Lady**
- 18 **More Than an Actress**
- 21 **Role Model**
- 22 **Super Stats**
- 23 **Glossary**
- 24 **Read More**
- 24 **On the Web**
- 24 **Index**

From Shy to Stardom

Zendaya was a shy kid. She didn't want to try anything. But then she did! She first sang to an **audience** at age six. It made her feel good. This shy girl grew to be an actress and a music superstar.

ABOUT THAT NAME!
Zendaya's dad picked her name. He put zen with the **Shona** word *Tendai*. It means "to give thanks."

Zendaya goes by just her first name. Her full name is Zendaya Coleman.

Zendaya's mom worked at this Shakespeare theater in California.

Bit by the Acting Bug

Zendaya helped at a theater where her mom worked. She liked seeing the actors. She wanted to try acting. In sixth grade, Zendaya played a silkworm in *James and the Giant Peach*. She loved it.

Chasing Her Dream

Zendaya loved to watch Disney Channel. She dreamed of being a star. At age 12, she moved to Los Angeles with her dad. This made it easier to **audition** for acting parts. She was in local plays. She got modeling roles and took dance classes.

MAKING A CHOICE
Zendaya's parents played basketball. They thought she might like it. She was good at it. But she wanted to act.

Zendaya started her career as a child model.

Zendaya poses with her *Shake It Up* co-star, Bella Thorne. They played dancers on the show.

Finding Fame

Zendaya landed her first TV role at age 14. She was on Disney's hit show, *Shake It Up*. She guest-starred in other TV shows, too. At 16, she starred in Disney's *Frenemies*. Her dream to be a star came true!

Music Star

Zendaya can sing! In 2011, her first song, *Swag It Out*, was recorded. In 2013, she released an album. Her hit song, *Replay*, was on it. As a child, her voice was quiet. It grew strong and brave with time.

DID YOU KNOW?
In 2013, Zendaya was the youngest dancer on *Dancing with the Stars*. She was 16 and got second place.

Zendaya is a talented singer and songwriter. She has performed songs live and in movies.

Zendaya is known for her beautiful red carpet looks.

Leap to the Big Screen

In 2017, Zendaya was in *Spider-Man: Homecoming*. This was her Hollywood movie **debut**. On-screen, Spider-Man caught her. In real life, Zendaya does not need a superhero. Her own talents make her famous.

A SWINGING ACT
Zendaya played a **trapeze artist** in the movie musical *The Greatest Showman* (2017). She did most of her own stunts.

In 2022, Zendaya won her second Emmy for *Euphoria*.

Leading Lady

Zendaya landed her first **lead** in 2019. It was in the HBO TV series, *Euphoria*. She won two Emmy Awards for her role. She was the youngest actor to do this. She keeps trying new things.

More Than an Actress

Look around. Zendaya is everywhere. She's in movies and musicals. She dances and is a fashion **icon**. She wrote a book to give advice to teen girls. There is even a Zendaya Barbie doll.

DAYA FASHION
Want to walk in Zendaya's shoes? Slip into some Daya shoes. The fashion line is named after her childhood nickname.

Zendaya believes in body positivity. She has spoken out against body shaming.

Zendaya likes to take time to meet and talk to her fans.

Role Model

Zendaya grew up to be a confident woman. She is a performer who uses her voice in many ways. She sings and acts. She also speaks out against bullying and racism. Zendaya stands up for what is right.

NEWS FLASH
TIME magazine put her on their 2022 list of 100 most influential people in the world.

SUPER STATS

ZENDAYA MAREE STOERMAN COLEMAN

Birthday: September 1, 1996

Birthplace: Oakland, California

Home: Los Angeles, California

TV Roles: *Shake It Up* (2010–2013), *K.C. Undercover* (2015–2018), *Euphoria* (2019–)

Main Movie Roles: *Spider-Man* movies (2017, 2019, 2021), *The Greatest Showman* (2017), *Dune* movies (2021, 2024), *Challengers* (2024)

AWARDS

Emmy Awards: 2020, 2022

Golden Globe: 2023

Critics Choice Awards: 2023

MUSIC

Replay (2013)

Rewrite the Stars (2017)

All For Us (2019)

GLOSSARY

audience A group of people gathered to see or hear a show or game.

audition A tryout for a performing part.

debut A person's first time performing.

icon A person widely known and respected for having influence in a certain sphere.

lead The main part in a movie or play.

trapeze artist Someone who does stunts in the air on a trapeze bar.

Shona A language of the Shona people of Zimbabwe.

READ MORE

Anderson, Kirsten. **Who Is Zendaya?** New York, NY: Penguin Publishing Group, 2022.

Poux, Jennifer. **Zendaya.** New York, NY: Grosset and Dunlap, 2020.

Schwartz, Heather E. **Zendaya.** Minneapolis MN: Lerner Publishing Group, 2022.

ON THE WEB

Britannica Kids
https://kids.britannica.com/students/article/Zendaya/634758

Ducksters
https://www.ducksters.com/biography/zendaya.php

Kiddle
https://kids.kiddle.co/Zendaya

INDEX

awards, 16, 17
bullying, 21
dancing, 8, 10, 12, 18
Euphoria, 16–17
fashion, 14, 18
modeling, 8, 9
roles, 10–11, 15, 16–17
Shake It Up, 10–11
Shona, 4
songs, 12–13, 15

About the Author

Mary Bleckwehl is a children's author who loves cookie dough and talking to kids. She is happiest when she is biking and exploring new places. Mary lives in Minnesota with her husband and monster dog. Check out her books at marybleckwehl.com.